A GUIDE TO
TELEPATHY AND PSYCHOMETRY

A GUIDE TO
TELEPATHY
AND
PSYCHOMETRY

(The Laws of Thought Projection, and The
Scientific and Practical Aspects of Psychometry)

By

S. G. J. OUSELEY

Author of—" The Science of the Aura "

LONDON
L. N. FOWLER & CO., LTD.
29, LUDGATE HILL, E.C.4.

PRINTED IN GREAT BRITAIN
BY W. & J. MACKAY & CO., LTD., CHATHAM

CONTENTS

PART I. TELEPATHY

CHAPTER   PAGE

    I. THE SCIENCE OF TELEPATHY 9

   II. HOW THOUGHTS ARE TRANSFERRED ... 14

  III. TELEPATHIC PHENOMENA 19

  IV. PRACTICAL METHODS OF DEVELOPMENT ... 24

   V. THOUGHT-FORMS AND EMANATIONS ... 31

  VI. CREATING AND PROJECTING THOUGHT ... 36

 VII. THE PROJECTION OF THOUGHT-FORMS ... 43

PART II. PSYCHOMETRY

    I. THE NATURE OF PSYCHOMETRY 55

   II. THE PSYCHOMETRIC FACULTY 61

  III. PRACTICAL DEVELOPMENT 67

  IV. COLOURS AND SYMBOLS 74

   V. HUMAN PSYCHOMETRY AND PREDICTION 81

PART I

TELEPATHY

PART I.   TELEPATHY

CHAPTER I

THE SCIENCE OF TELEPATHY

THE five senses—sight, hearing, smell, taste and touch—have been described as the Five Gateways of Knowledge. They are the usual avenues through which come all our impressions regarding the outer world. The range of these so-called " physical senses " is very limited.

All impressions, external as well as internal, are vibrations of some kind. The power of the eye, for instance, to register the luminous vibrations of the ether is extremely restricted. Beyond the normal range of vision in the Solar Spectrum there exist vast scales of finer vibrations which our eyes cannot register. Only a limited range of mechanical vibrations of the air reach the membranes of the ear. The dimension of space, or solid, opaque, or non-porous objects, render the organs of sense powerless to assist us.

In spite of the limitations of the physical senses there have been men and women in all ages who have possessed superior or super-normal senses and faculties, enabling them to push aside the frontiers of matter and to contact the finer, subtler vibrations of the universe. Whether we call them seers, prophets, adepts, Yogis, or sensitives, they are simply demonstrating a power that exists in embryo in every human being—the power of the individual mind to link itself to the Universal Mind.

The power or faculty of the human mind to absorb the thoughts of another brain and to project its own thoughts

9

irrespective of time or distance is one of the attributes which is shared with the Universal Mind. Former generations regarded such a power as " supernatural "—today it is regarded as a purely natural function.

In the materialistic Victorian era stories such as the *Corsican Brothers*, Scott's *Waverley* and *Legend of Montrose*, were looked upon as impossible outside of fiction. Since then there has been no lack of evidence to show that two people in sympathy or affinity with each other can communicate their thoughts when far apart ; that a son dying in the Burmese jungle can convey his last wishes to his parents ; that the contents of documents sealed and secured under lock and key can be read correctly.   In America, Major Buckley developed 148 persons so that they could read sentences shut up in boxes or nuts.*

The materialist does not admit these powers because he is imprisoned within the limits of his physical senses. To him there can be no information or knowledge except through the usual channels of sensation and perception based on the activity of the brain-cells.   The occultist knows differently.   He is aware of other gateways of sensation, profounder avenues to knowledge.

The facts of Psychometry, Clairvoyance and Telepathy in themselves prove the falsity of the materialist view. The deeper we probe into the psychology and complexity of the human personality the more the evidence for supernormal faculties is brought to light.   We have to realise that within each one of us, there are potentialities that far outstrip normal intelligence and transcend the limitations of sense and, indeed, of even the time-and-space dimensions.   A vast universe of experience exists beyond our normal consciousness. The "threshold of sensibility"—the limits of sense-perception—is not insurmountable.   Occa-

* See Babbitt's *Principles of Light and Colour*, p. 528.

sionally in inspiration, in dream, in intuition and in hypnotism, the threshold is moved and the human spirit moves temporarily in worlds not realised by the senses.

It is in the emergence of the dormant interior Self that there come into operation these higher, wider and deeper powers. One of the best known and most attested manifestations of the Higher Self is seen in the phenomena of telepathy. We owe the term telepathy to the great metaphysician, Dr. F. W. H. Myers, who introduced the word in his famous book, *Human Personality*. He defined it as " the communication of impressions of any kind from one mind to another, independently of the recognised channels of sense." Literally, it means " far-feeling."

Previously, telepathy was known as thought-transference, which was made a subject of popular interest by Sir William Barrett as long ago as 1876, when he read a paper before the British Association, in which he suggested that a committee should be formed to investigate the possibility of ideas being transferred from mind to mind, independently of the ordinary channels of the senses. This resulted in the founding of the Society for Psychical Research in 1882, and which, from that date to the present day, has been ceaselessly collecting and examining cases of telepathy and correlated phenomena. Though reserved and cautious in their conclusions, the members of the society have compiled and published records of enormous value to the psychic student.

The results of the earlier transactions of the society are embodied in *Phantasms of the Living*, the result of the investigations of Myers and his associates. In this book the authors establish, with a prodigious amount of carefully-collected evidence, the existence of a hidden faculty or subconscious self as well as the familiar conscious self with which we think, reason, perceive, etc. Myers termed this inner principle the *subliminal self*. Through it we express all the mental and psychical activities which manifest beneath the threshold of normal consciousness. It may be considered as a sort of " unconscious intelligence " containing not only the record of all past impressions and experiences but also possessing powers and functions far transcending the range of the conscious self. Like the invisible radiation of the sun, it is invisible and yet all-important.

Whether we designate the higher mental powers by such terms as the subconscious mind, the sixth sense, the intuitive faculty, the subliminal consciousness and so on, the fact remains that there is a thought-force, an intelligence working within our own organisation distinct from that of our conscious personality. The science of physiology shows that the development, nutrition, and renewal of the body and brain, which occur automatically and unconsciously within us, are beyond control of our conscious minds.

Many explanations have been brought forward to account for the cause and phenomena of telepathy. Some consider that it is caused by some emanation from the brain, a form of mental radio. Others say that it is due to a radiation of the aura or an etheric projection. The earlier philosophers advanced the doctrine of the Universal Mind which lies behind the mind of the individual and links all together.

The majority of investigators have favoured the theory of radiant energy in some form as the main factor in telepathy. We are surrounded by vibrations and cosmic forces at all times although we are normally unconscious of them. These higher forces act as the media for the transmission of thought and feelings irrespective of distance or time.

Thus the power known as the Reflecting Ether, flashes upon our consciousness from time to time fragmentary impressions and sensations from the Universal Mind. May not the same agency convey our thoughts and feelings independently of the channels of the senses ?

Podmore, the great psychical investigator, was unable to decide whether the faculties involved in telepathic phenomena were but the germ of a higher power latent in man, or whether they were the last vestiges of a power becoming defunct by disuse—" crowded out and forced down below the threshold by the cares and distractions of our workaday consciousness."

So far as is known at the present time there is no sense organ or mechanism under the control of the will that produces telepathy. It is known, however, that certain sense organs exist in the lower orders of animal life the use of which is problematical. In human beings also every anatomist knows that there are certain vestigial organs, the precise purpose or use of which is a mystery.

For example, situated in the bony cavity called the " Turkish saddle," between the brain and the roof of the mouth, is a tiny gland or organ called the *pituitary body :* another small gland, the *pineal*, lies behind the third ventricle of the brain.

According to occult teaching, these two glands are not mere vestiges. They belong to a class of organs which in the average person of the present day are neither degenerating nor developing—they are dormant. In the remote past the pineal gland and the pituitary body were active centres of clairvoyance and also thought-transference.

In the epoch of evolution called Polarian, the pineal gland was a highly sensitive organ of feeling corresponding to our organs of sight and hearing which were then only in a rudimentary state. It is worth while recording that modern ethnologists admit that savages possess some form of telepathic power which possibly advancing civilisation has put out of use.

B

CHAPTER II

HOW THOUGHT IS TRANSFERRED

THE Science of Telepathy is based upon the Science of Mind and the laws of thought. To many people the term "thoughts" merely signifies the result of intellectual activity—the ideas evolved by the reasoning faculties. But the term is capable of a much wider and deeper interpretation, and any study of telepathy, the art and science of thought-manipulation, would be abortive without a thorough understanding of the real nature of thought. The mere recital of cases of telepathy and thought-transference, interesting though they be, are apt to grow tedious as they throw but little light on the principles involved.

A thought may be considered as any mental state or mental activity, including those of the intellect, feelings, emotions, will, desire, imagination, or memory. The states we term feelings, desire, will and imagination have a degree of tangibility more pronounced than the states of pure ideation or intellectualism. The former type of thoughts are *creative* in essence while the latter are abstract processes based upon the images, ideas or concepts created by the first named set of mental activities.

The dynamic power or force of the preceding set of mental states is much greater than those of the purely intellectual operations, because they are more elemental, basic and formative, and because they involve more psychic energy and soul-force than abstract intellectualism.

Thought is a force and its products remain as forms in the reflecting ether long after the person who expressed them has ceased to live. As the images of things which exist in the reflecting ether remain there for aeons they may be contacted by the psychometrist and the tele-pathist. Thus, it will be seen that thoughts are *substantial* things—real tangible products of energy and will.

Why is a " thought " termed a " thing " ? Because Mind itself, the birthplace of thought, is a substantial form of energy. The universe is the manifestation of Divine Mind. Mind is static energy—thought is dynamic energy. Hence it follows that mental energy is capable of producing effects even at a distance by means of vibratory thought-waves. An idea conceived in the mind is a vibration and can be propagated or radiated from the brain in currents and waves.

The relation between thought and telepathy will now be seen more clearly. It should be realised that there are several kinds of telepathy which can roughly be classified into three main types :—

1. Telepathy between persons who are in mutual sympathy or affinity.

2. Telepathy between persons having no connection or link with each other.

3. Telepathy which is voluntarily induced from the agent to the percipient who may or may not be a stranger, but upon whom the agent is deliberately experimenting.

In experimental telepathy there is a transference of a mental image of certain words, figures, designs and various symbols, from one mind to another. This transference, of course, involves the radiation of thought-waves : but in such cases the mental image transmitted is almost always some conventional, abstract idea such as certain words, names, numbers, or diagrams, that have very little emotional power and which are in consequence, very difficult to transmit. The fact that they are trans-mitted at all, even under exceptional circumstances and, between people in sympathy with each other and with the advantage of the particularly sensitive organism of the receiver, is proof of the power of thought-waves and mental vibrations.

Many people have underestimated the importance of telepathy and have discounted its universality owing to the admitted difficulty of reproducing these delicate tests involving the transmission of abstract symbols and requiring unusual powers of receptive sensitivity. The frequent failures of laboratory tests and public exhibitions of this kind causes many people to look on telepathy as something " abnormal " and " unusual." And yet the commonplace fact is overlooked that everyone receives similar thought-waves from others which affect each individual according to the character of his own thought.

There will certainly be few people who have never experienced the truth and reality of telepathic impressions. Most people, for example, have on occasions suddenly sensed the approach of some person previous to his or her appearance, or have unexpectedly thought about a friend a little before a letter arrives. Who has not " felt " the pain or distress of some loved one at a distance ? Such experiences are too common and universal to require argument, but it will at once be seen that the majority of them are cases of reproducing the emotional states of consciousness in other minds rather than the transmission of mere words or abstract symbols.

Telepathy is more likely to occur when it concerns the condition we call emotive or subconscious. As an example of telepathy between two persons in sympathy with one another, the case quoted by Dr. Boch of Munich, just before the Second World War, is interesting. On one occasion he became suddenly conscious of a relative who was about to undergo an operation in a particular room in a hospital which he recognised—he was aware that the lady was wearing a piece of blue ribbon. Knowing that another room, which the patient had preferred, had been ordered for her, he rang up the hospital to inquire if the lady was in the original room. He was informed that this room was not available as the patient still occupying it could not be moved. Later on he called to see his relative and found her lying in the room which he had seen in his vision—she was wearing the blue ribbon. It seems quite probable that the lady, upset at being put in the wrong room, subconsciously sent a telepathic message to him.

The waves of thought arising from special mental states are projected far beyond the body according to their nature and intensity. A person of strong feeling and emotion, will or imagination, has a tendency to project his thoughts a great distance. Examples and methods of the projection of various thought-forms are given in a later chapter.

Cases of telepathy between persons having no connection with each other are quite common. One such case will suffice to illustrate this point. The two principals of a private school in New Brighton, Miss A., and Miss B., were sharing a bedroom, and in the morning Miss B., on waking, told Miss A. that she had had a most vivid dream in which a woman came to her and said : " There has just been a murder at the Victoria Hotel and the murderer slept in your house." The particular hotel was directly opposite the school. Some three weeks later, while the two ladies were together at Eastbourne, Miss A. came to her friend one morning with a copy of the local paper, exclaiming : " Here is the explanation of your dream ! " The paper contained an account of the shooting of a maid employed at the Victoria Hotel, by her sweetheart. At the inquest the dead girl's brother gave evidence that the man had threatened to kill her because she had jilted him, showing that the murder was premeditated. Here it seems reasonable to suppose that in some manner Miss B.'s subconscious mind received a telepathic communication from that of the murderer as he was planning his crime.

Intense concentration of thought and feeling flows out from the thinker's mind and impresses the reflecting ether which exists everywhere and thence it may enter a receptive mind. Whether a thought-vibration reaches another mind or not it is bound to leave an impression on the ether and may be sensed at any time.

As we see in the science of psychometry, every event that takes place on the physical plane is recorded in the memory of nature. The thoughts and pictures imprinted on the reflecting ether react upon the mental spheres of individual minds and can create in them emotional disturbances or a vague awareness even if these pictures do not come to the full consciousness of their minds.

It should always be remembered that thoughts and ideas tend to become living entities with an independent existence. A thought set in motion in the reflecting ether resembles the expanding ripples on the surface of a lake— a thought projected to a given destination by a powerful mind may be compared to a ray of light passing with atomic-velocity through the ether of space. The power of some people to detect and receive mental-projections is much greater in some than in others.

Some interesting investigations into voluntary telepathy were made by Rudolph Tischner assisted by his colleague Dr. Wasielewski. The telepathist was a young lady, Miss X., who was quite unknown to Tischner and only slightly known to the doctor. Miss X. was placed in a chair in front of a big writing-desk which was enclosed in a large folding screen covered with a thick rug that formed a roof and hung down the sides of the chair making it impossible for her to see through the chinks of the screen.

The two men retired to an upstairs room where they chose the objects for making the test. They then returned to the room where Miss X. was still seated in the " cabinet " and kept the chosen objects carefully concealed from her : these consisted of a shaving-brush, a pair of scissors, a violin and a small flask. Miss X. was able to name all but one, the shaving-brush, correctly.

CHAPTER III

TELEPATHIC PHENOMENA

THE Society for Psychical Research has been collecting cases of telepathy and conducting scientific experiments for over half a century. Each case is carefully examined and reviewed from every angle. The number of cases stamped with the society's imprimatur amounts to several hundred. All serious students of the subject should study the Proceeding and the *Journal* of the *S.P.R.*

I propose in this chapter to give a few typical cases. The following example is mentioned in the *Journal* (Vol. VI, p. 129). A certain Canon Bourne and his two daughters were out hunting and the girls decided to return home with the coachman whilst the Canon went on. " As we were turning to go home," say the two Miss Bournes, " We distinctly saw father waving his hand to us and signing us to follow him. We all three recognised both him and the horse. The horse looked so dirty and shaken that the coachman remarked that there must have been a nasty accident. As father waved his hat we clearly saw the Lincoln and Bennett mark inside, though from the distance we were apart it should have been impossible to have seen it. Fearing an accident we hurried down the hill. Owing to the nature of the ground we lost sight of father, but it took us very few seconds to reach the place where we had seen him. When we got there there was no sign of him nor could we see anyone in sight at all. We rode about for some time looking for him in vain. We all reached home within a quarter of an hour of each other. To our surprise father then told us that he had never been in the field at all the whole of that day. He had never waved his hat and had met with no accident.

In this case the telepathic factors at work are obscure. No accident had happened to Canon Bourne. It can only be surmised that some involuntary emanation, such as the projection of the psychic double of the Canon and his horse on the reflecting ether, had been sensed by the two girls and the coachman who were sensitive to such impressions.

Telepathic impressions are not confined to the waking consciousness but sometimes take the form of dreams. Thus a Miss Mann, of Cambridge had a vivid dream that her old friend, Dr. X., whom she had not seen for ten years was sitting beside her asking why she had not been to see him. The following morning she told it to her husband at breakfast. She had no reason to be thinking of Dr. X. at the time, but a few days later she heard that he had died on the morning following her dream.

A vivid impression of two friends whom he had not seen for twenty-eight years, nor had any correspondence with them, occurred spontaneously to a man one Sunday morning. A few days later he read in the paper that on that very Sunday morning Mrs. C. (his friend's wife) had been burned to death through her nightdress catching fire.

To gain a right perspective of telepathy the investigator gathers together and compares as many telepathic examples as possible and then considers whether there might be any other explanation. This involves much tedious and laborious work as witness the forty or fifty volumes of the Society for Psychical Research. The general conclusion arrived at by the scientific investigators seems to be that while telepathy is a fact, the why and wherefore is still problematical. In the majority of cases chance or coincidence are ruled out. Whatever the cause of the phenomena, the part played by the subconscious mind in causing telepathic visions and awareness is very important.

Telepathic impressions appear to stimulate the subconsciousness of the percipient and to cause a disturbance or some activity there which gives rise to a visual manifestation and so forces the impression on to the conscious mind.

In my own life I have had several personal experiences of telepathy, some quite trivial, like seeing a person in a dream and then receiving a letter from him the following morning : others of a far different nature such as dreaming of a room with a group of relatives and friends and a clergyman in the centre. A week later I received news of the serious illness of my mother from which she did not recover.

Another time it was a case of telepathy plus foreknowledge. I was interested in a new literary venture, a psychic magazine that was going to be produced by a rather affluent young man who was a new convert to Occultism. The young man's real interests were decidedly material and I had grave doubts as to the ultimate success of the venture. However, the young man was most enthusiastic and nothing seemed to deter him. One morning I felt an urge to write him regarding the seriousness of the project he had in view, and suggesting that he postponed it for a time. Something cropped up that made me forget to post the letter. The next morning I heard from the young man that he had decided to abandon the idea altogether !

On another occasion I had a particularly vivid dream. I was in a desolate tract of land like a desert which was cloaked with heavy mist or smoke. Whilst the mist drifted and curled about a part of the ground began to swell and heave and presently a most beautiful temple arose and sent out strong rays of light which soon cleared away the smoke and mist. A lady to whom I related this dream a week or so later told me that she had had exactly the same dream at about the same time.

These simple cases serve to illustrate how closely we are all linked to one another in the world of thought—the inner realm of consciousness. We are constantly sending out our own messages and receiving impressions from the Universal Mind as well as from individual minds.

Mr. G. N. M. Tyrell in his recent book *The Personality of Man*, quotes some interesting cases of spontaneous telepathy and foreknowledge. In one of these, the percipient, a lady who appears to have been subject to precognitive dreams at various times, had a curious dream in August, 1937, which she luckily recorded at the time. " I dreamt I was talking to a number of people in a street and saw A.A. (a friend of hers) through a gap in a broken wall sitting in the cellar of a house. Somebody said something about ' 10th May ' and I said : ' That is very significant and I will remember that date.' "

On 10th May, 1941, A.A.'s house received a direct hit from a German bomb and was completely destroyed except for the basement. The man was not there. It is interesting to note that although the house was destroyed as seen in the dream the man was not in it. He evidently appeared in the dream simply to indicate to whom the bombed house belonged. The facts of this case make chance-coincidence quite improbable—the day of the month was given and the dream occurred three years and nine months before the event. Incidentally, 10th May, 1941, was the date of a memorable air-raid on London.

On 8th June, 1943, the newspapers reported that a man had been mauled by lions at Whipsnade Zoo. On the previous night a certain Miss W. woke up suddenly and told her friend, Miss S., that she had had a terrifying dream in which she had seen a man mangled by lions in a country place. (See *S.P.R. Journal*. Vol. 29, p. 2.)

The last example shows that telepathy does not pre-suppose any special bond of sympathy between the people concerned.

The cases I have given exemplify the natural or spon-taneous manifestation of telepathy. These spontaneous cases afford the most striking evidence for the phenomena : nevertheless, the scientist, trained to examine everything by laboratory tests, is inclined to look askance at such natural cases because they cannot be observed or con-trolled. Experience shows that the telepathic faculty cannot be forced into activity, labelled or measured by experiments with cards, dice, screens or numbers. There is always an element of tension, of forcing or trying and at least hoping to attain results through sheer effort. This very probably defeats its own end through the lack of that spontaneity which appears to be a condition of true telepathy.

A few years before the war the B.B.C. in conjunction with the Society for Psychical Research carried out a large-scale experiment in telepathy. Over 24,000 people took part—yet, the telepathic results were precisely nil. The same may be said of most of the clinical experiments con-ducted " systematically " by psychologists and scientists. It should be noted, however, that some of the experi-ments carried out under rigid conditions by Dr. Soal and

Mr. Carrington in this country and by Dr. Rhine in America have successfully established the telepathic faculty.

Whilst believing that the faculty cannot be forced or made to work " to order " I am firmly convinced that most people can develop the power to a much greater extent than they are aware of by following the right methods of training. Many people have developed this power and in the next chapter I will explain some simple and safe methods to follow.

You will find that the faculty grows by practice and it should be remembered that the more you desire to know and demonstrate the great powers and truths within your being the closer they draw near to you. Everything depends on the right attitude of mind. Cultivate the expectant attitude, without strain, mentally excluding all external sense-impressions from the inner citadel of consciousness : then will interior perception and soul-sense emerge. It is when the outward sense of things is transcended and the submerged Self breaks through that the hidden powers of your personality become manifest.

CHAPTER IV

PRACTICAL METHODS OF DEVELOPMENT

It will be recalled that in Chapter III I wrote that two little-known glands in the cavity of the brain—the Pineal and the Pituitary—are, with their etheric counterparts, the probable cause of telepathy and other supernormal phenomena.

The goal to be aimed at in telepathic experiments is

the reproduction as far as is possible of the internal conditions and the psychical attitude that existed in those far-off days when certain faculties, which are now dormant, were part of man's normal equipment. Admittedly, it is not easy to re-waken latent forces, but the first and most important thing is to cultivate the right attitude.

The first thing to cultivate is the art of undivided, attention, or concentration. This implies thought-control, allowing the attention to dwell on only one idea or mental conception, such as peace, or contentment, and holding it there steadily. It is not allowing, for the time, any intellectual activity, except for one thought or mental concept. At the same time you must learn to relax, for strangely enough, a part of concentration is complete relaxation.

In telepathic development and experiments the room should be in partial darkness so that the eyes are stimulated as little as possible. This " darkening out " is necessary because in early epochs, when man used his inner senses as normally as we use our physical eyes, there was no light as we know it. The room should be as quiet as possible with nothing to distract the attention of either the percipient or the agent. The percipient must make his mind as calm and detached as possible, but should not try to produce a state of " mental blankness " which without arduous training, is seldom achieved by western people.

Quietness is necessary so that the organs of hearing do not function. You should sit in a comfortable chair, or recline on a bed or couch, so as to bring about a calm relaxed state of mind and body. Smoking must not be allowed, nor the use of strong scent or incense which will stimulate the sense of smell.

Nothing complicated should be used for the tests : select some ordinary object within the room, then when the experiments become more advanced obtain something from outside. A good method is for the agent to have various simple diagrams such as a triangle, a cross or a circle, concealed within a case or a drawer. The percipient is given a sheet of paper and a pencil and asked to draw whatever impression he gets.

Before attempting to practice telepathy the great requisite is perfect relaxation. The way to relax is to " let go." Let go of every tense muscle, every tense nerve in your body. Pain is tension. Pain can be inhibited by suggestion, followed by complete relaxation. Convey to your subconscious mind the message that you are going to function for a time in your higher mental body and you, therefore, wish to forget the physical body. You are going to concentrate on one idea and then completely relax consciousness. This is far better than trying to force yourself to make the lower mind a " blank." Letting go of the body implies letting go of the lower material mind. Practice this withdrawal until you feel completely relaxed bodily and mentally.

Some people find the following method helpful. Relax the body as completely as possible, then visualise a small disc of colour—choose the colour you feel most in harmony with. Gaze steadily, peacefully and restfully at the colour —feel it radiating towards you : think only of it. If you find that a circle of colour is too abstract for you to visualise, then turn to the mental image of a flower. Whatever object you choose be careful to avoid anything that is associated with distressing or unpleasant experiences. When you have found a peace-inspiring object just look at it with undivided attention. You must be on your guard not to let your concentration induce sleep, which would be an auto-hypnotic state, and is not the state for telepathy.

After you have practised the exercise of concentrating

on a flower or a colour you will have done something towards achieving control of the mind, which is absolutely necessary for successful experiments in telepathy. There may be a feeling of strain to start with, but it is getting rid of strain both physical and mental that constitutes perfect relaxation. Practice will teach you what this state is—after a while you can achieve it without strain.

Here is a simple exercise for telepathic development. Ask someone to draw half a dozen simple designs on cards or pieces of paper which must be folded so that you cannot see the contents. Each should be folded separately for handling one at a time. They should be placed on a chair or a table within easy reach of your hand. Remember to darken the room—if the experiment is to be made at night have a table lamp, or some light, near for turning on or off as required, without too much effort and without upsetting the passive state of receptivity which you should be in. Don't forget to supply yourself with paper and pencil.

When you have set the drawings on the table turn off the light and stretch your body full length on the couch or bed. Close your eyes and relax every nerve and muscle in your body completely. You should not consciously endeavour to make your mind a blank, as this effort will set up a counter-vibration—simply " let go " mentally. Don't think of anything. Make your mind passive without forcing or straining. It is essential to produce this passive state of mind and body—if the mind is not passive it feels physical sensations and vibrations. If the body is not relaxed its sensations interfere with the necessary mental passivity : each rests on the other. A few deep breaths may prove helpful as that has the effect of establishing a rhythm in the physical and mental bodies which will result in quietness and calm.

When you feel ready, and not before, take the first

drawing and hold it over the solar plexus : it should be held lightly without pressure. Your mind will now be quite passive and receptive. Calmly but positively *will* your subconscious mind to reveal to you what is drawn on the paper. Repeat the command several times in words such as these :—

" I require the contents of this paper to be presented to my conscious mind," or, " I want to see what is on this card (or paper)." Speak, mentally, as though you were addressing another entity. Then relax into perfect passiveness again for a few moments and endeavour calmly and gently to see whatever forms or mental images that may begin to build up. Keep your physical eyes closed as the perception belongs to your etheric organs.

You will probably see misty fragments of forms first— just a few faint lines. Sometimes a complete form manifests at once, swiftly photographed on the ether. These mental apparitions appear and disappear with lightning rapidity, never standing still until your consciousness is raised to the same rate of vibration. They never appear in heavy lines, but are characterised by an ethereal fineness. Beginners sometimes fail to observe them at all, but by dint of steady practice one becomes aware of them in the dim grey background of the mind. At times they seem to vanish, as it were, into the shadows. You should then endeavour strongly to recall the first vision—do not remain passive but exert your whole will-power to summon the thought-forms back again. Make a mental note of it so as not to forget it because the next step is to make the mind passive again.

You must deliberately blot out all forms and pictures from the conscious mind including the one that has just manifested. The subconscious mind should now be ordered not to present it to the conscious self again unless it is the *right* picture, the picture drawn on the card. Make the conscious mind blank for a few moments and then focus your inner eyes on the grey ether of mind for a vision. This is to test whether the first vision was a trick of the subconscious or whether it came from the reflecting ether, via the etheric sensory organ in the brain.

This process should be gone through two or three times and if the first manifestation persists on reappearing you should accept it. When you feel that it is the correct picture, turn on the light and without looking at the card or paper make a complete sketch of your mental picture. This is an important part of the technique as it is surprisingly easy to forget some part of a mental vision or to merely imagine the vision to be the same as the original picture. This method will not be acquired in a day or a week : it takes patience and training in the art of concentration. It is, however, a method that is in harmony with sound psychological and occult laws.

The above exercise can be used for private self-development as it does not require any other person except the agent who draws the designs or diagrams.

For mass-telepathy, an interesting experiment can be carried out with an ordinary pack of playing cards. Any number of persons can take part : those who are to transmit the messages are called the *Senders* and those who are to receive or register impressions are called the *Receivers* or percipients. The latter may occupy an adjoining room or a room upstairs as the case may be.

The person acting as the Displayer raises a selected card so that a good light falls on it. It is most important that each Sender sees it distinctly. To ensure this the Displayer should give a signal that he is about to exhibit the card—a sharp rap on the table will do. Directly the signal is heard the sitters should gaze at the card which should be on view for seven seconds and then hidden.

There are three things which a Sender must carefully

C

avoid. First, when you gaze at the card be very careful *not* to make the mind a blank. Secondly, do not hold the image in the memory, the doorway of the subconscious mind. Thirdly, you should not *will* that the Receiver shall get the message. These acts of the mind produce vibrations that will interfere with the centres of thought-transference.

It is essential that those who are acting as Receivers also adopt the same attitude. They should sit under the same conditions. The Displayer or his assistant should give a signal when the object is being displayed—a slight tap on the wall if the sitters are in an adjoining room. If the experiment is taking place in a different house the telephone could be used. Take care, however, to avoid any sudden or raucous sound that might have a shattering effect on the nerves.

The Receivers are given pencil and paper to record their impressions : as soon as they hear the signal they write down the mental image they receive. It sometimes happens that a Receiver will divine the object correctly just before the signal is heard—in other words he will be a few seconds ahead of time. This occurred frequently in the telepathic experiments carried on by Professor S. G. Soal of Queen Mary College, London University. One of the party persistently got the card correct, *one place ahead*. The same phenomenon was recorded by Mr. Dunne in his book, *An Experiment With Time*.

For an experiment of this kind ten objects at a time are quite sufficient—allow half a minute between each display. When the experiment is over the papers are at once collected and given to the Displayer who marks them right or wrong. A golden rule for a Receiver is ; " Record first impressions."

CHAPTER V

THOUGHT-FORMS AND EMANATIONS

" We are just entering what may be called the ' field of vibrations,' a field in which we may find more wonders than the mind can conceive."

MARCONI.

THE study of thought-forms and emanations is an interesting and instructive branch of mental phenomena. The very nature of the study has the effect of making the mind more sensitive to the super-physical world and is a considerable aid to students of telepathy.

From the psychological aspect, thought-forms are of fundamental importance in investigating the phenomena of the mind. The old conception of *thought* as something merely abstract, unreal and shadowy—vapour fancies, intangible dreams and imaginings—is given place to the belief that thought is a force, a substantial entity that can be moulded and directed by the will of the thinker. Thus, science today is turning to the view that the universe is a vast living thought-form of a Superior Will, manifesting as matter in varying degrees of vibration.

This is in harmony with the ancient teaching of occult science that everything in the universe is a manifestation of Universal Mind. Everything that exists, exists within the Universal Mind and nothing can exist outside of it because the Universal Mind includes all.

In spite of the scientific principles concerning Mind and the collected evidence as to its remarkable power and phenomena, many people still regard the term " thoughts " as implying something fanciful and idealistic—nothing more than the motions of the grey matter of the brain or the abstract activities of the reasoning faculties.

We have defined thought as any state of consciousness, or mental activity, including those of the intellect, feelings, emotions, will, desire, imagination, memory, or any other mental principle.

The psychological distinction between abstract and concrete thought is not denied. The mental phenomena associated with the feelings, emotions, desires, will and imagination have a degree of *force* more pronounced than the states of abstract intellectualism. The former class are creative and dynamic in their nature, while the latter are merely intellectual motions of the mind consisting for the most part of the formation of ideas, reasoning processes and such like.

The dynamic and projecting power of the first-named states of consciousness greatly exceeds that of the purely intellectual operations of the mind. By their very nature they are more elemental and primitive and as such are capable of generating more energy, and vibrational power thus infusing their characteristic thought-forms with more life, strength and intensity. The thought-forms for example associated with strong emotions like love and hate are far more pronounced and virile than those accompanying such abstract mental processes as are involved in pure mathematics, logic or philosophy.

The power and intensity of thought-forms vary according to the thinker and the type of mental activity. Broadly speaking, thought-forms may be classified under four main groups :—

1. Thought-forms connected with the character and personality. All during our life we are building up character and personality and are creating individual thought-forms in our magnetic atmosphere. Our character thought-forms

are our inseparable satellites. We carry them with us wherever we go.

2. Thought-forms connected with our ideals, life-aims and aspirations. Our habitual thinking creates thought-forms which tend to materialise. Our dreams, very often, are the forms or patterns of our inmost thinking and wishing.

3. Thought-forms connected with the fulfilment of our desires and wishes—the power of the mind to attract to ourselves the persons, things and environments with which we are in harmony. Science demonstrates that the vibration of a particular atom attracts towards it another atom of a similar vibration. In the same way our thought-forms exert a pressure and influence upon ourselves, and upon others in harmony with our vibrations.

4. Thought-forms that act like vibratory waves influencing those minds in vibration on the same plane, just as we are influenced by the thought-forms of others with whom we are in harmony. Mental vibrations are as tangible as etheric vibrations, electro-magnetic waves and cosmic radiations. Each kind of thought-form has its own particular rate, degree and character of vibrations. We attract our own kind of thought-forms to us—we repel our opposites.

We should realise that all our lives we are consciously or unconsciously attracting the vibrations with which we are in harmony.

From what has been said about the power and influence of thought vibrations it will be understood that *thought-forms are real things*—tangible entities, real forms of energy.

For corroboration of this, we have the modern scientific view of Mind as energy—Sir James Jeans has compared the Universe to a living thought-form, a vibration of Universal Mind. Mind is potential, static energy—thought is dynamic, vibrating energy. The energy manifesting as thought-forms produces effects, even at a distance by means of vibrating thought-waves.

The student will by now realise that a thought-form is a manifestation of energy, a vibration projected into the thought-atmosphere, or *aura* as it is more correctly called. which surrounds the human body.

The thought-forms emanating from particular mental states are projected to either greater or lesser distances from the thinker according to their nature and intensity.

The man or woman of strong mind and will, forceful desires and emotions, vivid imagination is able to project thought-forms to a great distance.

If anyone doubts the power of the mind to project forms then we would draw attention to the experiments of Dr. Baraduc of Paris. This famous French scientist actually projected thought pictures on to sensitive plates. He regards the invisible vibrations through which the mind projects its images as of the nature of light. Dr. Baraduc obtained various impressions by strongly thinking of an object—he used a sensitive plate to capture the effect produced by the thought-form. In one of his experiments he projected the face of a lady whom he knew and of whom he had once made a drawing—he held the thought-form strongly in his mind. Dr. Baraduc regards the creation of an object as the projecting of an image out of the mind and its subsequent materialisation. Among his experiments, was the projection of the vibration of a sincere prayer which appeared as a radiating force in the form of an expanding circle. Another prayer projected a form like the fronds of a fern. The thought-form of friendship appeared like a mass of greeny-blue rippling waves ; it was projected by three people who were close friends. A lady experiencing deep sorrow projected a form resembling a strong grey vortex.

Not only do individuals project distinctive thought-forms and auras but towns and cities, social bodies and communities, even countries and places have their collective thought-forms created, of course, by the combined thoughts of the individual units.

Every town generates its own distinctive atmosphere of thought. It does not require special sensitiveness to feel aware of the difference in character between a northern industrial town and a London suburb, or between a holiday resort and a university town. Buildings and streets have their peculiar atmosphere. There is a vast difference in the thought-forms associated with a church and a cinema, a public-house and a library. To the sensitive mind Oxford Street has a different vibration-atmosphere to Leadenhall Street—and so on.

We react to the thought-forms encountered in public buildings and places in two ways, viz.—Firstly, we absorb the vibrations which are in harmony with our own ; secondly, our expression of thought-forms is hindered or frustrated by the opposite thought-vibrations of others who do not think or feel on the same plane as ourselves.

Thought-forms, like material bodies, not in mutual harmony or sympathy, clash.

In the first case, the law of *affinity* operates, attracting to a person the thought-forms and objects of an harmonic vibration with himself, and repelling inharmonic vibrations. The second case calls into operation the law of *opposites*, which manifests by tending to oppose, resist, and obstruct the expression of opposites, states and forms.

In view of these facts, it behoves us to control our thoughts so that we attract to ourselves only the thoughts and mental vibrations conducive to our well-being and advancement. Thus if we generate thought-forms of grief, worry, depression, hatred, we are bound to attract similar forms emanating from the minds of others which will aggravate and increase our own mental condition.

If you walk into a room, or along a street, with your aura darkened by negative thought-forms, you at once draw to yourself the same dark influences from other minds similarly afflicted, whilst at the same time you shut out from your thought-atmosphere the uplifting and helpful vibrations that you would otherwise receive. Avoid people and places that affect you adversely as you would avoid the plague. Seek and cultivate people whose thought-forces correspond with your own. The Bible advice—" Be strong in the spirit " means, in the language of occultism, the cultivation of strong, positive, thought-forms which will absorb the detrimental forms and vibrations from other minds, just as certain substances absorb unwanted and detrimental rays of light by manifesting their own colour of expression. The law of mind is that positives absorb negatives.

CHAPTER VI

CREATING AND PROJECTING THOUGHT

THE next point to consider is the second effect of thought —the creation of a form. This aspect of the subject can only be understood by referring to the vital substance known to the eastern occultists as Akhasa and to western students as elemental essence.

This is the primordial semi-intelligent life-substance which pervades all space and is the animating principle of the mental and astral planes. Condensed by the organising power of the soul it clothes the forms of the latter and renders them visible on the physical plane. This substance is highly sensitive to the influence of human thought and every impulse from the astral and mental bodies manifests itself as a form composed of the vital substance. Temporarily the thought so expressed exists as a living entity consisting of a form or body (the elemental essence), and a life-principle or soul (the thought force).

Such thought-forms, or elementals as they are sometimes called, appear in a vast range of shape and colour.

It may help students to conceive of thought-forms as electric batteries—the vehicle of vital essence being symbolised by the container and the mental energy by the electricity. When you concentrate your thoughts and feelings upon someone else or upon some definite object or aim the thought-form can be projected towards the desired goal.

The aura of every person and thing can be impressed by *images*—a thought-form is a mental or astral image which is projected through the ether to affect the aura or " senses " of the receiver. When your thoughts concern yourself or are connected with some personal feeling they remain in your aura ready to present themselves to your consciousness at any given moment.

A man, for example, is subject to envious feelings regarding a neighbour who possesses an expensive car, an attractive wife, a nice house and other worldly assets. Whilst engaged at his daily work he may push the worrying thoughts out of his mind even though the associated thought-forms are hovering in his aura like a dark cloud ; his attention, however, is absorbed by his tasks and his astral body does not react to any other rate of vibration. At the cessation of his labour, when the rhythmic vibration of interest ends leaving his mind " open " he will most likely feel the sensation of envy taking hold of him. Instead of shaking himself out of the negative condition by

directing his attention elsewhere he reacts to his own
thought-forms.

No man can hope to escape from the confines of his own
aura or thought-atmosphere. We live and move about
surrounded by the mass of mental and astral forms of our
own creation. Our aim and purpose should be to people
this vital thought-atmosphere with inspiring, congenial
and radiant forms instead of harbouring a collection of
dark, cloudy, misshapen entities.

Through his thought-atmosphere a man views the world
and the people about him. He sees life tinged with the
predominant colours of his aura. Thus it is hardly possible
for anyone to see and judge things as they really are unless
well-balanced control of the mind and emotions is first
achieved.

Besides the thought-forms we have just described there
is another large variety which cannot be classified as
definitely personal nor as directly objective. They are
better described as the products of vague thinking which
" float " as it were in the ether, vibrating and radiating
according to the original impetus that launched them into
space. Except when it merges into some other mental
body, the radiation gradually diminishes until nothing is
left of the form. Floating forms of this type sometimes
impinge on a mental body in a sympathetic rate of vibration and become absorbed by it.

The creation of forms by vibration can be demonstrated
by the science of acoustics. If a brass or glass sounding-
plate is covered with fine sand and is then gently rubbed
on the outer edge with a violin bow, the sand is thrown
into the air by the vibration and falls back on the plate
in specific patterns and lines. If the plate is touched at
different points different vibrations are produced and
varying forms of remarkable precision and symmetry are
obtained. Similar phenomena occur with voice-forms. All

these facts demonstrate the power of the mind to visualise thought, to create thought-forms and to bring them into objective manifestation.

From the form-aspect of thought we may classify the phenomena into three groups :—

Group 1. The form that takes the aspect or image of the thinker. When you mentally visualise yourself in some distant place or strongly desire to be there you create a thought-form of your own image which is projected there. This type of thought-form may become visible to others and is sometimes taken as the astral form of the thinker— a projection of the astral body. In this case, however, it is necessary either for the receiver of the thought-impression to be naturally clairvoyant or for the thought-form to be sufficiently strong to materialise.

The mind from which such a definite entity emanates will also have great determination and strong will-power.

Group 2. The form which takes the aspect of a material object. For example, in thinking of a friend or some. person you create in your mental body a miniature image of that person—if well-visualised the form will manifest in your mental aura (externally) and appear before you. This is not a magical phenomenon but merely the projection of a simple thought-form. When " imaged " in your aura the form will usually appear surrounded with characteristic colours which symbolise certain thoughts emotions and mental states—the subject of colour-symbology is very interesting and will be dealt with in the next chapter.

In a similar way to the foregoing you form in your mind miniature images of objects—houses, places, scenery— which are also projected into your aura. The things, too, you desire—the things you have longed for but have failed to attain—these all have to be moulded, formed and projected into your aura before they will materialise. The forms of the things you desire, the money you want, the position you aspire to, must be moulded first from mental and astral substance and strongly projected as a vibrating, living portion of your soul. Remember that only strong, vibrant and radiant thought-forms will attract, or link up with, the objects you are seeking. A well-expressed thought-form is like a magnet.

Thoughts have an inherent tendency to materialise objectively. A strongly expressed thought-form by striving to evolve into being on the physical plane sets into motion the Law of Attraction and also calls to its aid the subconscious activities of the mind—the mental machinery that supplies the power for carrying out a desire or project.

Actually there is nothing magical or specifically occult about the materialisation of thought. A moment's reflection will enable you to realise that all human creative inventive, artistic, and even technical work is simply the logical result of the manifestation in material form of ideation and imagination. Every material object built or constructed by man first existed as a thought-form in the mental body of an individual. Every house and piece of furniture has had its invisible thought-form in the mental aura before appearing in physical matter.

A strongly-expressed thought-form is already half-way towards objective manifestation. The great leaders in science, art, invention, music, commerce, having once formed their initial ideas, clothed them with soul-substance, infused them with energy and brought them into visible manifestation.

It would of course be foolish to deny the fact that many fervent wishes, longings, aspirations, and ideals fall short of expression and materialisation. But it can be confidently asserted that the main reason for failure is the fact that the majority of people ignore or lack some or all of the following conditions :—

1. Absolute clearness concerning what is desired.
2. Strong visualisation.
3. Mental energy or impelling power (Will).
4. Strong magnetic radiation.
5. Well-built and clearly-pictured thought-forms.
6. Vital contact with the subconscious mind.
7. Right use of the auric vibrations.
8. Effective projection.
9. Continuous desire.

The man who achieves his purpose is first fully clear and definite about what he is seeking and is filled with a continuous and concentrated desire. The desire reinforces the will (impelling power) and helps the imagination (image-making or visual faculty) to create strong effective pictures. Without strong desire and effective visualisation it is impossible to create clear and vital thought-forms. On the other hand the strongest desire and most resolute will cannot accomplish anything for the person whose mind lacks a clear mental picture or image of the thing he wants.

The thought-form must be built or projected into the aura wherein it is held and strengthened by strong magnetic radiation. Your subconscious mind plays its part by filling or sustaining your thought-form with a constant supply of desire-force. You must feel a longing and yearning for it—this attitude will set into motion the laws of the thought-world which will tend to materialise your thought-form.

Once you start the right laws working within you will be surprised at the new vitality in your mind—new ideas, new angles, new methods will open up in your consciousness. You will attract the right persons, things and environment conducive to the materialisation of your thoughts.

Group 3. The third class of thought-forms consist of

those which take a definite individual form, expressing their own essential qualities. Forms of this type usually manifest on the astral plane—they are expressions of feeling as well as of thought. The specimens of typical thought-forms which are given in the succeeding chapter belong almost exclusively to that class.

It is interesting to note the effect of thought-forms directed towards individuals—the effects may be partially reproduced in the aura of the individual or may be repelled from it. It is not difficult to project a thought-form of love and protection towards some person by first concentrating on the thought and visualising it, then *willing* it to enter the aura of the person. It will remain there as a protecting influence, seeking all opportunities to serve and defend by discharging the impulse impressed upon it. It will augment beneficient forces that impinge on the aura and will obviate harmful or maleficent ones.

Healing thoughts sent out in " absent treatments " are effective for the same reasons. It is important to remember that when good or evil thoughts are projected at individuals such thoughts must find in the aura of the recipient the right conditions for responding sympathetically to their vibrations. In other words if the thought-form finds no congenial or similar elements present it can have no effect on that aura ; instead it rebounds from it and returns to the sender.

People who fear hostile psychic influences need have no fear of them if their minds and hearts are good and pure. When an evil thought strikes the aura of such a person it cannot cause harm or mischief but must rebound from it following the magnetic lines of least resistance, that is, it seeks the projector who then suffers the injurious effects he intended to bring about. " The evil man becomes his own victim " is an ancient Hindu saying of undoubted truth.

CHAPTER VII

THE PROJECTION OF THOUGHT-FORMS

THOUGHT-FORMS are based on the inner harmony and affinity existing between form, colour, vibration and mind. These four inter-related powers are at the back of all phenomena, and by right concentration and training, the student can utilise and employ them in his life. Any strong mental emanation may result in a thought-form.

Figuratively speaking, a thought-form is an etheric message, embodied in a definite shape, and ensouled with life and colour. Thought-forms usually build up in the aura, as though a veritable part of it. Some exceptionally strong emanations, however, present themselves as separate entities.

To start with a simple but fundamental form—the emanation of Peace and Protection. There are many times when we wish to send thoughts of love, peace, and protection to friends, and others from whom we are separated. We first enter the Silence, making ourselves as relaxed as possible in body and mind. With the elemental essence of our mind we mould an image of two spreading wings joined together by a disc. That is the shape of our Peace and Protection form—not unlike the winged disc of the ancient Egyptians. The form is then ensouled with living luminous colour—a beautiful rose-red for the wings, expressive of tender affection, and a disc of glowing gold, symbolising the power of mind. Keeping this image in our consciousness, we concentrate on the friend we wish to help; and after thirty seconds, release the thought-form through the ether-charged space. To infuse still greater force into our mental projection, it is helpful to express with our lips some such phrase as " I send to so-and-so thoughts of peace and harmony. This exercise in thought-form building may be repeated six or seven times. Remember that for a thought-form to be effective it must be clearly pictured, rightly coloured, and animated with sufficient mental energy—there must also be present an intense desire in the mind.

The goal of a projected thought-form is the aura of the recipient, where it will either be partially reproduced or repelled. The clairvoyant faculty has revealed many examples of thought-forms connected with the feelings, passions and other psychological phenomena. A typical phenomenon is the thought-form of *dreamy* affection. This appears to the clairvoyant eye as a somewhat vague, misty or nebulous cloud of a warm rosy hue. It emanates from the minds of persons whose thoughts are calm, tender and loving in regard to a friend. The feeling is pure and unselfish, but a cloudy blurred shape in the form indicates that it lacks power and effectiveness.

In some cases the thought-form of love and affection contains undesirable elements. When the bright carmine of love is rendered dinghy by the presence of dull brownish-grey, it is an indication that selfishness of some kind has crept in. A high degree of thought-form is seen in the manifestation of intense affection such as that shown by a mother for her child. There is the formation in the aura of a crescent shaped vortex tapering at the ends, and glowing with a luminous crimson light. It is a beautiful phenomena, and the brightness of the colours indicates the purity of the emotion and thoughts behind it ; whilst the definite character of its outline shows the vital intensity which animates it. Such thought-forms of pure affection are projected into the auras of the loved ones.

The thought-form of brotherhood and universal love is

a spectacle of great splendour and beauty. These formations emanate from advanced souls—people who are in unison and harmony with the great soul of the Universe. They present the appearance of a glowing orb or circle of a brilliant rosy-red colour, with innumerable rays pointing in all directions. The living light emanating from such glorious forms appears to proceed from within like an inexhaustable fountain. This magnificent thought-form lights up the aura with a radiance of indescribable beauty.

Glancing again for a moment at the lower manifestations of feeling, there is a type of thought-form which is best described as animal or brute-like. It belongs inherently to the lower astral plane. It is seen in the auras of stunted, low-grade souls, and indicates only selfish propensities. It is a form composed of dark lurid rays which, in contrast to the straight radial lines of universal love, are crooked and hooked. Instead of turning out in all directions, they are bent in upon themselves. The dull heavy tints bespeak selfishness and sensuality. The sad plight of such souls in their vain pursuit of happiness is seen in the fact that the curving hooks reflect back upon themselves.

A little self-sacrifice and service for others would swiftly transform this negative thought-form into a radiant star of divine love and harmony.

The thought-forms connected with spiritual aspiration mystical and religious sentiments are varied. In most cases they glow with a luminous blue light of varying depths and shades. The person vibrating on the spiritual plane has usually a large amount of luminous blue in his or her aura. Around the heads of people in prayer or meditation are seen thought-forms of blue. In the case of vague indefinite thoughts and ideas—such as emanate from the minds of the majority of church-worshippers—the blue thought-forms are cloudy, misty and very indistinct. Frequently there are brown and grey streaks

D

present in the auras, the psychic reflection of selfishness and fear. This, of course, is the wrong attitude in which to approach the Infinite, yet the presence of such thought-forms at least indicates the beginning of spiritual aspiration, albeit the wings of real devotion and wisdom are absent.

The thought-forms accompanying the more thoughtful and intelligent souls in prayer and meditation are far more developed and distinct. With them is seen a slender round cone, tapering to a point emitting a very luminous blue radiation. This is very different from the cloud-like blurred thought-form of ignorant devotion. The thought-form of purposive and directive devotion is a spire of developed spiritual power—not a wavering formless sentiment. The aura is lit up with a pure bright radiance— the radiance of spirit. In true spiritual development there is an uprush of power, whilst the clearly defined form manifests the quality of the concept, and the clearness of the colour is evidence of the inner feeling.

In the thought-form of meditation the mental power of the thinker converges in a single point of concentration, whilst the shaft of the former is rooted deep in the mental body or the higher mind.

Even more glorious than the blue cone of meditation is the response from the spiritual spheres. The Infinite Power is always ready to pour through when the soul is attuned, just as the light of the sun is waiting to stream down on the earth when the sky is clear. The Divine Power is seen clairvoyantly as a concentration of irridescent rays of singular strength and purity which surround and impregnate the spiritual thought-form. " The golden light of Spirit shoots its effulgent beams on the disciple. Its rays thread through the thick dark clouds of matter, like sun-sparks light the earth through the thick foliage of the jungle growths." (Voice of the Silence.)

On every plane the Infinite Spirit pours forth Light, Power and Life. But it is on the higher planes of being that the Divine Radiance chiefly affects—the mental plane rather than the astral, and the spiritual and intuitional plane more than all. Yet there are conditions under which the power appropriate to a higher plane may be transmitted to a lower one. This happens when a bridge, as it were, is created between the higher and lower worlds —when the thought or feeling is devoid of self, so that the energy, instead of being bottled up in the senses, is freely liberated, and thus does not turn back again into itself, but penetrates to the higher world. By thus establishing contact a true spiritual thought-form makes a bridge so that the Infinite Power can pour *down* into the lower planes of being with potent results for the thinker and others. This inflow of divine Light is the true spirit of inspiration, healing, intuition, and higher wisdom. It leads to a higher state of consciousness in the originator of the thought-form.

Thought-forms emanating from the intellect or mental body have a yellow or golden radiance. The yellow ray in the aura is the gauge of man's intellectual capacity. There are many shades of yellow, but as a general rule, the appearance of dark, dull tints signifies vibrations of a material nature. When self-interest is the main concern, the auric emanation is a yellow ochre. This is widely present in the auras of most business men and salesmen, whilst scholars and others engaged in the pursuit of philosophy or science have a clear golden radiance in their auras, which may gradually assume a luminous yellow or primrose colour, glorious to behold. Yellow thought-forms are usually distinct and clear—the definite manifestation of intellectual pleasure and appreciation.

Whenever the mind is engaged in pure intellectual gratification, such as the contemplation of a great work of Art or the hearing of a piece of beautiful music, the yellow cloud is present in the aura. The thought-form of mental inquiry or the state of mind concerned with seeking knowledge is a characteristic and interesting type. Slender rods or rays of a bright golden colour build up in the aura, showing thought and reflection. A person when asking questions with a genuine desire for knowledge exhibits the same form. The more intense the desire for knowledge, the brighter and deeper the golden hue in the aura. Sometimes these thought-forms of inquiry change into spiral shapes. In cases of mere curiosity the thought-forms are not illuminated with the golden hue of intellect, but are a dull brown colour.

A common and well-defined thought-form that frequently occurs among certain types of business men and politicians is seen in the orange hooks of power and ambition. Rich orange is the colour of ambition, and the curving hooks which are seen extending forward only are symbols of desire. This form is not undesirable if the intention is high and noble—the presence of selfishness, however, will be recognised by the clouding of the orange with dull reds, browns and greys.

The difference between thought-forms of the praiseworthy ambition type and the narrow selfish type is not only in the colour but also in the shape. Selfish ambition presents a floating dull-hued form surrounded with ugly misshapen projections like talons of acquisitiveness. The impression conveyed is a general tendency to grasp everything in sight.

The study of thought-forms, as the students' power of clairvoyance develops, becomes of increasing interest. In all departments of life, at work, in the home, at social gatherings and functions, the thoughts and emotions of people are continually giving rise to the appropriate forms and symbols. Some people, quite unconsciously, emanate delightful, uplifting and inspiring thought-forms, whilst with others—and these are generally the majority—the very reverse is the case.

The minds and emotions of people in the presence of Death are excellent guides to character and the condition of enlightenment or ignorance. Some very interesting thought-forms are to be witnessed at such a solemn event as a funeral. The rites attending the burial of the dead produce various effects in the auras of different people. Clairvoyantly speaking, there are two broad types of mourner, viz.: those who are in a state of ignorance, fear or superstition concerning death, and those who are enlightened by a knowledge of the occult facts regarding the cessation of life in the physical body.

The thought-form of the man to whom death is something hideous and dreadful appears as a vague, dark, earthly cloud, entwined with bands of brown and leaden grey, with a dark tapering appendage which seems to descend into the grave itself. The psychic emanation is one of hopeless depression, fear and horror. As he gazes at the grave it is a grim reminder of his own inevitable decease. The dark earthy clouds in his aura typify the desire to escape from an unknown fear. The dark leaden bands are produced by the desire to hold on to the physical body, and the downward appendage indicates a desire to bring back the dead man to the physical plane.

The contrast to this gloomy condition, the thought-form emanating from the man whose mind is enlightened by true knowledge presents a very different picture. In lieu of the dark and cloudy emanation, we see a clear-cut, bold and beautiful thought-form, expressing sane and balanced feelings. Instead of the tapering appendage tapering downwards, there is a slender cone pointing *upwards* surrounded by a circle of golden stars. The cone of feeling is highly coloured in accordance with the emotions felt—a rose-red in the lower part indicating love and affection, blue in the centre expressing devotional feeling and violet in the upper portion, denoting spiritual serenity and calmness regarding a necessary stage in human evolution, notwithstanding the apparent grimness and grief of the occasion. The golden stars are expressions of spiritual aspiration towards the higher planes of life. The thought-form emerges from a circle of leaf-green colour, a sign of deep sympathy and understanding, and a band of deeper green showing the mental and spiritual harmony.

One of the most beautiful and expressive thought-forms is that seen in the aura of two friends on meeting again after long separation. It is crescent-shaped, and is composed of three sections of colour—one horn is rose-red, radiating gladness and affection, the other horn is a delicate nil or pale green, the colour of sympathy, the middle portion is shining gold, indicating the mental pleasure which the reunion causes.

So far we have dealt only with the more pleasant types of thought-forms, with the exception of the negative form seen at a funeral. There are, unfortunately, a great many ugly, foul, depressing and hideous emanations which also manifest in the auras of people. A few examples will suffice to make this negative and undesirable type of thought-form clear. The feeling of anger and intense resentment gives rise to a most unpleasant and repellent picture in the aura. Anger has the effect of *exploding* the auric elements, the discharge depending upon the intensity and quality of the feeling. In a sudden outburst of anger against another individual there appear pointed shafts or dagger-like shapes of burning red. The head of the shaft is often hidden in a dark reddish-brown cloud, indicating the blinding, smothering feeling accompanying the angry passion.

These ugly shafts flash out on all sides of the aura, and

with every outburst there is a corresponding loss of etheric energy. Scientists state that passions like anger and hatred have reactions in all the glands of the body.

In the form of anger arising from fury or irritation without the element of sustained hatred the aura bursts into particles of a fiery red and orange hue. A more intense and furious form of anger occasions a thought-form shaped like a scarlet disc, with sharp rays flashing outwards.

The mind and will, it should be remembered, are the determining factor in the power and intensity of all emotions. In people of strong and imperious wills, the thought-forms of anger appear so vivid and powerful as to pierce the surrounding atmosphere, and seem to act like a murderous force on the object of their wrath. Another very common but unpleasant thought-form appears as a snake-like shape of a brownish-green colour. This is seen in the aura of jealous-minded persons, the twisting, serpentine shape indicating the watchful, anxious attitude of the person concerned. The symbol of jealousy is frequently seen to change into a second shape in which the emotion of anger is present. It appears as a dark murky cloud, out of which shafts of red vehemence continually project. These fiery flames appear ready to strike at the imagined enemies.

An exceeding painful thought-form is that expressing fear and fright. The aura appears to be breaking up, as though hit by a tidal wave. When actual terror is present dark blurred patches of grey float in the aura, out of which emanate quivering grey lines of fear. The auric atmosphere is charged with discord and intense anxiety. When the clogging and paralysing feeling of terror is absent the expression of fear is exhibited by crescent-shaped etheric fragments of a pallid grey colour, which are thrown out from the auric envelope like eruptions of lava. The appearance of the fear thought-form suggests that the man is seeking to defend himself by projecting these etheric fragments, despite the fact that in doing so he is really wasting strength and energy. At times, scarlet tints also appear, showing anger and indignation.

The thought-form of avarice or selfish greed has a characteristic shape. It is represented in the aura as a claw-like form projecting from the astral or desire-body. The colour varies according to the exact amount of envy which accompanies the desire for possession, but it generally has a muddy green hue, showing both jealousy and deceit. The waving tentacles of greed curl, and stretch in the direction of the object desired.

The power and actuality of these mental emanations is well described by Annie Besant in her book, *Karma*. "The life-period of these ensouled thought-forms depends first on their initial intensity, on the energy bestowed on them by their human projenitor ; and secondly, on the nutriment supplied to them after their generation by the repetition of the thought, either by him or by others. Their life may be continually reinforced by this repetition, and a thought which is brooded over, which forms the subject of repeated meditation, acquires great stability of form in the psychic plane. So again thought-forms of a similar character are attracted to each other and mutually strengthen each other, making a form of great energy and intensity, active in the astral world.

Thought-forms are connected with their progenitor by what—for want of a better phrase—we must call a magnetic tie ; they react upon him, producing an impression which leads to their reproduction, and in the case mentioned above, where a thought-form is reinforced by repetition, a very definite habit of thought may be set up, a mould may be formed into thought will readily flow—helpful if it is of a very lofty character, as a noble ideal, but for the most part, cramping, and a hindrance to mental growth."(*Karma*,p.17.)

PART II

PSYCHOMETRY

PART II—PSYCHOMETRY

CHAPTER I

THE NATURE OF PSYCHOMETRY

Occult science teaches us that every material object has its history recorded upon it in the ether which interpenetrates and surrounds everything.

The intuitive or clairvoyant description of the etheric record is technically called *Psychometry*, or soul-measuring.

Everything in Nature has mind and memory, which is preserved and manifested in the aura indefinitely. This peculiar power or property is known by some occultists as the *reflecting ether*. This is not a force but rather an inert, passive substance which underlies the more active forces familiar to us, such as electrical-phenomena and more especially radio-activity. It is capable of taking up the vibrations of those bodies to which it is related and which it invests. Of itself it has no active properties but in its still, well-like depths it holds the potentiality of all magnetic forces. Like a sensitive photographic plate the Reflecting Ether takes the pictures of every moment and holds them in its grasp. The Egyptians knew it as the Recorder. Among the Hindus it is known as the *Akhasa*, which gives rise to the term the *Akhasic records*. Paracelsus called it the " sidereal light " which later became known as the " astral light." Modern scientific investigators approach it when they speak of luminiferous ether and radiant matter.

Whether we call this remarkable property of nature the Reflecting Ether, Cosmic Mind or Memory, or any other term, the fact remains that a record of everything we do and every thought we express is preserved in our mental aura and transmitted to everything we use or with which we are closely associated. By the medium of psychometry everything pertaining to our life—history, character, thoughts, emotions and even our essential potentialities can be seen and described in the common articles which we touch and handle.

Dr. Buchanan, the American scientist, who first investigated Modern Psychometry* stated after thirty years' study of the subject, that a good psychometrist could reveal a whole life's history and that nothing could be concealed. This statement is in accord with the ancient teaching of occult science that Nature has provided a means of universal and eternal memory which nothing can efface or destroy.

Psychology teaches that we virtually forget nothing. The subconscious mind, the seat of memory, is the indestructible storehouse in which all memories and impressions lie dormant. In the same way, through the etheric and intermolecular forces of our being, these memories are grafted upon the objects we use, the clothes we wear, and the rooms we inhabit. Such *impressions* and memories are locked up, as it were and preserved in the reflecting ether.

It is interesting to note that the life-history and memory-aura of inanimate objects which have not previously been associated with human beings can also be demonstrated by psychometry. Rocks, stone implements and weapons, buildings, relics, furniture, clothes and scores of other common-place articles yield up their secrets. The psychometrist taps these memories and reveals their past. " Every stone, every plant, every animal, as well as every man," says Dr. Hartmann in his book *Magic*, " has a sphere in which is recorded every event of its existence.

* The science was well known among the Ancients.

In the astral light* of each is stored up every event of its past history and of the history of its surroundings ; so that everything, no matter how insignificant it may be, can give an account of its daily life, from the beginning of its existence up to the present to him who is able to read. A piece of lava from Pompeii will give to the psychometrist a true description of the volcanic eruption that devastated the town and buried it under the ashes, where it remained hidden for nearly two thousand years. A piece of the bone of a Mastodon teaches the vegetable and animal life of antedeluvian periods."

A psychometrist, J. Cleary-Baker, writing in *Prediction* (Nov. 1937) says : " Through the agency of a chipped flint implement I obtained a most interesting glimpse of the New Stone Age. I found myself looking at a rough stockaded hut at the gateway of which sat an old man dressed in some kind of a skin robe. He was engaged on the work of chipping flints one of which I knew to be that which I held in my hand. And so I followed the history of the specimen from the time when it was fashioned to the time when it was lost during a hunt for wild fowl in the marsh."

A similar instance is reported by Professor William Denton. He once gave a psychometrist a small package containing a piece of lava. Concentrating a moment with the package in her hands she at once began to describe a volcano down the side of which a torrent of molten matter was flowing. She finished by exclaiming, " *Why, the specimen must be lava !* "

A fragment of a meteor handed by the same scientist to a psychometrist caused her to cry out, " It carries my eyes right up. I see an appearance of misty light. I seem to go miles and miles very quickly, up and up. Streams of light shine from a vast distance."

* A synonym of the Reflecting Ether.

There are countless similar cases which have been investigated and proved. Any article—a lock of hair, a piece of clothing, a letter—which a person has touched, handled or worn will indicate to a sensitive mind through its inherent and accumulated vibrations that person's state of health, his physical, emotional intellectual and moral attributes and qualities.

The explanation of the remarkable phenomenon of psychometry is to be found in the aura. A knowledge of the nature and functions of the aura is indeed a perquisite for the proper understanding of psychometry.*

Speaking concisely, the aura is a subtle emanation generated by the etheric and other forces of the being or object with which it is connected.

Everything in nature generates its own aura, atmosphere or magnetism. The fact is equally true of the lowest crystal and of the living organism of the lowest and of the highest conscious entity.

In the human organism there are forces analogous to, if not identical with, the forces of electricity and magnetism. Each human being possesses a magnetic field, which is the aura—it radiates from each individual as solar rays emanate from the sun. The human aura partakes of the essential qualities of the etheric, the astral, the mental and the spiritual forces of the individual. In a vital sense, every human being creates his own magnetic atmosphere which unfailingly reveals the temperament, disposition, character and health.

This auric emanation has been known to occult scientists for a long time under a variety of names. It is the " magnetism " of Mesmer, the " electric fluid " of Jusseiu, the " odylic flames " of Reichenbach, the " vital rays " of Dr. Baraduc, the " human atmosphere " of Dr. Kilner.

The researches of these men of science prove conclusively

* See *Science of The Aura*, by S. G. J. Ouseley. Fowler & Co.

that all bodies, whether animate or inanimate, emit a subtle radiation. If this were not so psychometrical readings would be impossible. Figuratively speaking, our thoughts and memories overflow and radiate until a thought-aura or atmosphere is projected around us. This thought-aura contains all our history and truly reflects our state of consciousness on all planes of being.

The power-volume of the aura varies in different persons. In people with strong mental faculties or intense emotional natures the thought-aura extends about nine feet. In those of mediocre mental capacity and weak emotional instincts the aura extends a much shorter distance, whilst in imbeciles there appears to be no demonstrable thought-aura whatever.

An important factor in the intensity and extent of the vibrations connected with the aura is the state of the subject's health. Any form of bad health reduces the strength and vitality of the aura and its vibrations.

It is through the medium of the thought-aura that objects receive the impressions and memory-fragments which the psychometrist recovers and describes. As the human aura radiates in every direction and impresses all and everything within its orbit, it is not essential that an object should be worn or used before it can become charged with an aura of its own.

For instance, you may have observed how some churches, particularly old cathedrals, impress you. No sooner do you cross the threshold than you become conscious of a feeling of sanctity, a spirit of reverence and awe, which seems to permeate the whole atmosphere. You feel refreshed and inspired by the aura. The reason for this, of course, is that the accumulated thoughts and prayers of generations of worshippers have hallowed the very walls, leaving on the reflecting ether an indelible impression.

It will thus be seen that psychometry implies two things. First, it implies that material objects can become charged or impregnated with the thoughts, feelings and mental aura of the people connected with them. Secondly, that sensitive people, when in a receptive condition, can " tune-in " to those impressions and recover the life-history of any article. In the case of churches, the only life that a church knows is an expression of mental, devotional and spiritual life. If thoughts register themselves permanently on matter then old churches will radiate those impressions. The very atmosphere of peace and calmness which hangs over the sacred building induces a passive and receptive state of mind. The conditions are therefore ideal for psychometry and so it is not surprising that even materialistic people are often strangely affected when inside a church. Not only buildings, but furniture, rooms, clothes, cities and countries accumulate auric impressions from the minds and souls of people closely associated with them. The psychometrist, by using his inner faculties, contacts the impressions and describes them.

The mental aura has seldom been better vouched for than in the statement of Dr. Mayo, a former professor of physiology to King's College Hospital : " I hold that the human mind is always to some extent acting exo-neurally or beyond the limits of the human body and that its apprehension extends to everything and every person around it."

That every human being is surrounded by his or her individual vibrations or emanations is further exemplified by the fact that it is no more difficult to psychometrise a person than it is to psychometrise an article.

Psychometry is a wonderful power and its possibilities are infinite. It extends to the past and can unveil the future. It is a relic of the past because it links us with a period when human evolution had not yet evolved specialised sense organs such as eyes, ears and nose. The only channels of sense perception were through the skin. It unveils the future because it foreshadows a time when our material observations will become augmented by information obtained through our psychic senses.

The faculty has been employed in the diagnosis of disease and many people have found it of great value in business life.

It is a power that can be acquired by nearly everyone and in the succeeding chapters we will show how it can be developed.

CHAPTER II

THE PSYCHOMETRIC FACULTY

MANY people are under the impression that the phenomena of psychometry is produced by the agency of discarnate spirits. In reality nothing is further from the truth. Whilst admitting the existence of external intelligences, it can be fairly and soundly stated that the psychometric faculty is not dependent on, nor does it normally work through forces other than those which are inherent in the human mind.

Psychometry can be developed by anyone with the right sensitivity of mind. The idea that it is *ipso facto* a form of mediumship is an error based on ignorance. Although properly termed a human faculty, nevertheless it is linked to the divine in man like every other expression of higher consciousness. It is an outworking of the divine

E

powers in man, but is not necessarily something super-rational or unearthly.

The faculty has been compared with mental medium-ship because the type of mind which is susceptible to psychometric impressions is akin to the mentality which manifests mental mediumship. There is the same degree of sensitivity and the same awareness of impressions from without. The great point of difference is, however, that the trained psychometrist is fully self-conscious of the psychic phenomena of which his awakened inner faculty is the source and origin.

I have frequently heard the question asked—is there any inner organ or faculty that produces the phenomena of psychometry? So far as is known at the present time there is no inner centre or nerve-mechanism under the control of the will for producing the phenomena. Every anatomist knows, however, that there are certain vestigial organs in the human body the precise purpose or use of which is a mystery. For example, between the brain and the roof of the mouth there is a minute gland or organ called the *pituitary body*—another small gland, the *pineal* lies behind the third ventricle of the brain.

Medical science knows little about the nature and function of these glands beyond the fact that they belong to the ductless group of glands and that they probably have to do with sex and physical growth and development. Some authorities dismiss them altogether as atrophied glands. According to occult teaching these two glands are not mere vestiges in atrophy. They belong to a group of glands which in the average person of the present day are neither degenerating or developing—they are dormant. In the remote past the pineal gland and the pituitary body were centres of clairvoyance and quite possibly they contribute in a greater or lesser degree to the faculty of psychometry. In most people these higher sense-centres are inactive but by development and the exercise of will-power they can be re-awakened.

With respect to the pineal gland, common medical opinion is that it is an " atrophied third eye." It is an ancient teaching of occult science, however, that the pineal gland is the centre of all psychical activity and that it is the medium by means of which we " see " or visualise on the super-physical planes of life. This would account for the phenomena of psychometry, astral visions, clairvoyance and the like. Geoffrey Hodson, in his *Science of Seership* mentions that through the medium of a highly-developed " third eye " he is able to diagnose diseases accurately and to analyse cultures, diluted to the thirteenth potency, enclosed in small glass tubes.

Few people can hope to reach such a degree of proficiency but whatever be the form of super-natural insight to be developed or undertaken, the one essential requirement is *sensitivity*.

By our thoughts, habit of living and mental attitude we can do a great deal towards attaining a sufficiently high degree of sensitivity. By turning our thoughts inward, we shall acquire the condition of consciousness requisite for undertaking psychometric exercises as explained in the next chapter. The great feature in psychometry is that the practitioner is really entering temporarily into the realm of consciousness surrounding the object being psychometrised. For the moment the psychometrist " feels " or " senses " all the emotions and conditions experienced by the other being or object. In the words of Dr. Buchanan, "The influence of a highly charged article is sometimes sufficiently strong as temporarily to charge the natural character of the psychometrist." The emotional impressions may be very intense—as in an article possessed by someone who has passed through, or *is* experiencing deep grief or anxiety. In such cases the psychometrist may be so overwhelmed by the "conditions" as to be unable to continue with the article. From the example, it will be realised that psychometry may be as great a curse as a blessing unless it is kept under proper control. Your wireless-set would be intolerable if it were continually operating. In the same way, if your psychic senses were continually picking up all and sundry impressions from the reflecting ether, your life would not be an enviable one. All supernatural forces have to be kept under proper discipline.

One sometimes meets people who are unconscious psychometrists. Some people, especially women, of a highly impressionable nature, react strongly to certain persons, places and things in a way which is wholly unaccountable to them. They go to look over a new house which seems all right at first, but they become conscious of a "feeling" that disturbs or upsets them. "I don't know why," they say, "but there is something about the place (meaning the aura) which I don't like."

They have unconsciously collected the thought-atmosphere of the previous occupants which the walls still retain. Thoughts are things—lasting entities that have a tremendous power for good or bad.

As the psychometric capacity is an extension of the ordinary mental faculties, it follows that the power to psychometrise is latent in every human mind. There are, of course, other qualifications that are necessary to make a good psychometrist.

The student of this fascinating science should be well-equipped mentally and in sound physical health. A natural sensitivity to super-physical vibrations and influences is a prime necessity—a great deal, however, can be done in this direction by patient cultivation provided the subject possesses a receptive responsive mind. Women, in whom the power of intuition is usually greater than in men, generally make proficient psychometrists although there are many excellent ones among men.

The female mentality and constitution is in general more receptive to psychical influences than the masculine character. But a great deal depends on training and the right mental attitude.

A wide general knowledge is a great asset, as in the course of psychometric practice one is carried mentally to various parts of the world and without a knowledge of geography a psychometrist will be limited to saying vaguely " I feel I am somewhere abroad " or " I am being taken north, south, east or west." Sitters require details !

In the same way, a psychometrist knowing nothing about history or physiology, will be at a loss to describe impressions coming from the past, or impressions regarding the body in disease. An elementary knowledge of anatomy and the organs of the body is a great advantage.

The phenomena of psychometry are not lifeless and colourless like an ordinary photograph—colours in all their glory are presented with the psychometric scenes. A knowledge of colours is quite essential, both in respect of their artistic significance and also their occult or esoteric meanings. Colour interpretation is a science in itself and the author has felt it necessary for the guidance of psychometric students to set down the occult meanings of colours in a later chapter.

It cannot be too strongly emphasised that a strict regard for fact and accuracy in psychometrising any article is of the utmost importance. The student should be on his guard not to be carried away by the " impressions " he is receiving, and not to exaggerate or overrate some peculiarity about the object which he admires or to which he feels greatly attracted. Care must also be taken not to be harsh or bitter in describing some impression which one dislikes or despises. A well-balanced mind is the *sine qua non* of good psychometry. Make it a maxim to understate rather than overstate.

It is beneficial for the beginner to observe good psychometrists at work. Follow their technique closely and afterwards you will be in a better position to criticise your own efforts, taking it for granted that you will be honest with yourself ! A good psychometrist, after holding an article, is able to get swiftly *en rapport* in his mind with your aura and vibrations and will proceed to state some facts about your health condition, illnesses you have had, your mental state, your habits, hopes, fears, and thoughts, your main business and social interests, your " pet ideas " *and* your prejudices. He will describe past incidents and journeys (even journeys you intend or contemplate in the future), people you know or have known and their apparent character. This will, of course, be based upon *your own* estimate of their character and personality.

If after about twenty statements, some fifteen or sixteen are correct then the psychometrist is one who is worthy of the name ! A proficient psychometrist is seldom wrong in dealing with the past or present but, statements regarding the future will have to be carefully remembered and proved. *Predictive* psychometry is a special branch of the science and will be considered later on in the book.

Psychometrists say that there is much variation in the speed or force with which articles present their memory auras and impressions to the mind. The reason for this is that the mental force of the people owning the articles determines the force and intensity of the aura around them. Every individual has his or her own " charging-rate " or wave-length. A man or woman in the prime of life with strong mental, physical and emotional auras, will impart a deep and intense thought atmosphere to the objects with which they are in contact.

CHAPTER III

PRACTICAL DEVELOPMENT

AFTER some time has been spent on studying the *rationale* of psychometry, the student should have sufficient knowledge and confidence in himself to begin practical development.

Two or three people with whom you feel in harmony should be sought to assist in the experiments. They should not be close or intimate friends as the less you know about their personal affairs the better it is for training your psychometric faculty.

It is important that you start with " one vibration " articles—that is, articles that have been in close contact with one person only. As we have already seen, the psychometrist has to deal with the aura of an object. The aura surrounding an object is of two kinds—firstly, there is the *inherent* memory-aura, and secondly, the accumulated aura. The inherent memory-aura is the object's own vibrations—the private store house of its own separate life. Accumulated memory is the sum-total of the vibrations that have been grafted on to it by its association with the human mind. A gold ornament, for instance, has a memory of its geological surroundings and associations before it was refined and shaped by the goldsmith—that is its inherent memory-aura. It also has impressed upon it the memory-aura acquired during the years in which it has been in contact with a human being—this is its accumulated aura.

Some psychometrists have a special aptitude for describing the inherent aura of objects, such as pieces of coal, lava, rocks and pebbles from the sea. Do not be surprised, therefore if in psychometrising a wooden pencil you become conscious of a thick, dark forest !

Before commencing psychometry the hands should be washed—preferably in warm water. Dry your hands on a cloth kept for the purpose—not a towel used by other persons. Cold hands are not good conductors of vibrations. It is equally true that very cold objects are difficult to " read."

The best results are obtained in a warm room and a slightly warmed article. The hands should be rubbed rapidly together before taking hold of an article.

Some authorities, including Dr. Buchanan, recommend gently tapping the forehead just above the root of the nose—the pineal gland, the source of the etheric " third eye " is thereby stimulated.

The experimenter should be comfortably seated with the arms resting on the arms of the chair. The sitters should be quietly seated and should not disturb the vibrations by talking or whispering. If there are a number of articles on a tray or plate take care that they do not touch one another—allow a few inches between each article. The psychometrist must not know who the owners of the various objects are.

Before attempting to " get " impressions from the article, you must endeavour to calm and still your mind by shutting out all thoughts and mental activity as far as possible. Hold the article firmly in the right hand— not just loosely by the finger and thumb. Some psychometrists move it about gently, but the contact should not be broken.

Close your eyes to allow the cerebral centres of vision to function without external influences causing interference. In a short while you may begin to experience curious flashes of intelligence—fleeting impressions that have to be focused and studied before they become intelligible. Do not hesitate to state any impression you feel in the mind or body. The incident, scene, or emotion must be described immediately. If not recognised, do not be discouraged—sitters frequently forget items which they later recall.

Some psychometrists work on what is known as the *objective* plane, that is they perceive the aura-pictures some distance away. These dream-like pictures are impressions from the reflecting ether which extends sometimes as much as four or five feet round a person. It is just as though a film was super-imposed on the material objects in the room. With other workers, the psychometric phenomena is entirely subjective, consisting of mental impressions, visualisations, symbols, etc.

At the commencement of psychometric development the importance of working with "one vibration" articles cannot be over-emphasised. Objects that have passed through the hands of various owners accumulate mixed vibrations which, colloquially speaking, will give the novice a "headache." A person who, for example, has bought a fountain-pen or a piece of jewellery second-hand will know nothing of the previous owners. The psychometrist will be faced with the unenviable task of sorting out the various vibrations and memory-auras which have been stamped upon by former owners. The present owner will be unable to understand the "messages" and the reading will become a tangled mass of confusion.

It is important to remember that not only real and actual impressions are registered by, but also the thoughts, aspirations, desires, hopes and wishes of the owner are presented to the impressional centres of the psychometrist. Emotions experienced by the sitter are reproduced, the things the sitter has seen will be reflected in the mind of the "reader."

Psychometry is the key to the secret of the mind or memory of the owner of the object. Everybody has wishes and ambitions which they *hope* will materialise and they sometimes cause confusion to the psychometrist as they are presented to his impressional centre with all the vividness of items of fact. Thus in psychometrising an article for a man, a very handsome dining-room clock was registered and given as belonging to him. In reality he did not own it, but had *hoped* he would acquire it ! It was the property of the man's grandmother who had *promised* to leave it to him when she died. The thought had so engrained itself on this aura that the psychometrist got the impression that it really was one of his possessions !

Novices in the science are advised to proceed slowly and cautiously in working on an object. Undue speed is not a sign of great power but will most likely lead to false trails. " Professionals " who rush to get through a tray of articles in half an hour have a technique of their own which is sometimes of a doubtful nature. Psychic forms soon break down altogether under pressure.

The cardinal point of psychometry, namely, the receptive mental condition, must never be lost sight of—while the conscious mind and as far as possible, the subconscious mind, is inactive, the psychic faculty is able to work unhampered and so contact the " records."

With well-developed psychometrists the visual imagining is not colourless. The aura, compounded of varying colours, is seen in its full range. The occult interpretation of colours is an important branch of psychometry—a later chapter deals thoroughly with this interesting aspect.

Before passing on to the next article, it is advisable to smartly rub the hands together or rub the palms with a handkerchief in order to remove the psychic conditions remaining on the hands from the aura of the first article.

This will avoid confusion which mixed vibrations would occasion in dealing with another object. Close proximity to the sitters should also be avoided and the distance should be not less than four feet between.

It will be found that some objects are much more psychometrically " alive " than others. In some cases the difference is very considerable. For example, an article that has been long associated with a highly emotional person, or someone possessing a keen intellect, or a radiant personality will be embued with vital forceful vibrations. On the other hand, if the article comes from someone manifesting a low degree of mental, emotional or vibrating activity then the psychometric yield is equally poor.

In psychometrising an article, the more surface the hands contact, the more satisfactory are the results. Necklaces, for example, have much vibratory surface and usually make good articles for reading. Rings and similar small confined objects are less satisfactory to deal with. The best articles are undoubtedly those that are worn next to the skin as they are in the closest contact with the person's aura. The hardness or softness of articles does not seem to make much difference. A glove or a purse can be psychometrised as easily as a medal or a watch. Certain soft, washable articles, however, such as handkerchiefs, do not make good subjects for psychometry. The washing process diminishes the aura and memory of the objects. Keys are another class of articles which we do not recommend, as they pass through too many different hands.

Letters are a particularly good medium for using psychometry. It should be remembered, however, that letters, in the course of their transit, are exposed to numerous sources of contact affecting their own inherent and secondary auras. The best way to psychometrise a letter is to remove it from the envelope, thereby eliminating one source of external contact. Spread the letter open on a table (avoid looking at the contents, of course) and cover it with your hand at the same time inducing the passive mental condition. If you prefer, you can place the letter between the palms of the hands. Methods of procedure differ according to the person. I have obtained satisfactory results by merely resting the finger-tip on the signature.

If there is good *rapport* you will experience certain bodily sensations, or you will become conscious of scenes and impressions relating to the writer of the letter. Describe them as carefully and as detailed as possible. Pause occasionally to inquire of the sitter if the statements are correct or not. Do not feel discouraged if the sitter looks " blank " or is unable to follow your remarks. In letter-psychometry, the sitter has usually a limited knowledge of the writer which has to be taken into account.

Letters frequently reveal the character of the writer. The signature is especially useful in this respect. Apply the finger-tips lightly on the signature and note the impressions. One may lay open the door to a person's complete personality—his mentality, emotional nature, moral fibre, spiritual or material status; condition of health, etc.

In the course of psychometrising a letter or any other object, you will at times experience sensations and emotions quite unfamiliar to yourself. Sometimes they are pleasant and uplifting, at other times they are depressing and unpleasant. Remember that a psychometrist is an instrument that registers *all* impressions, whether they are to *his* liking or not. Do not be alarmed therefore, if in psychometrising an article which has been worn by someone suffering from severe shock or mental stress you take on these conditions yourself—you can easily get rid of them by dropping the article and rubbing the hands briskly together.

One of the most interesting departments of psychometry

is the reading of photographs. It is a demonstrable fact that they can be psychometrised by the finger-tips of a good sensitive. It seems to be immaterial whether photographs be right side or wrong side up, or upside down or not. Place a photograph of someone unknown to you in a clean envelope, and lay your finger-tips lightly upon it. Induce the passive mental condition and after a few moments, observe what impressions and sensations you receive. You should be able to state the sex and appearance of the subject, apparent age, clothes, posture, position in life, health, whether physically alive or not, whether married, and numerous other particulars.

According to occult science, photographs, pictures, statues and so forth, attract the astral soul of the person whom they portray.

Another interesting use to which the faculty of psychometry can be put is the psychometrising of rooms. The best method is to stand in the middle of the room, induce the receptive mental state, and note the influences and impressions which are presented to your mind. Rooms are permeated with auras or emotional atmospheres. It is better to close your eyes whilst waiting for the "influences"—later on as you gain in experience you will find that your psychometric sense can function quite readily with the eyes open. Scenes and visions relating to the past history of the room will pass through the mind in the same way as dream-phenomena occur.

When demonstrating your powers in a room it will be necessary to have somebody present who is familiar with the history of the room to corroborate (or deny your statements). The confirmer should stand not less than five or six feet away to negative the influence which his own aura may exert on your psychometrising. If a confirmer cannot be employed, ask a friend to accompany you and write down the statements you make.

Stand or sit as you feel inclined. It should be borne in mind, however, that standing is always to be preferred to sitting.

CHAPTER IV

COLOURS AND SYMBOLS

THE *colour* aspect of psychometry is a subject that can prove very bewildering to the novice and for that reason I propose to equip the student with the main essentials of this interesting branch of occult science. The significance of colours has long been the subject of research and inquiry by occult masters and in the east various schools of esoteric knowledge concerning colour has been in existence for centuries. In later days the theosophical writers, especially Mrs. Besant and Mr. Leadbeater have done much to promulgate the secret meanings of colour-vibrations among the people of the west.

Colour plays a large part in the human aura and it also enters the field of emanation surrounding objects used for psychometry. As the psychometric sense increases one becomes conscious of a mental impression of colour in the objects being handled. These colour-vibrations frequently refer, to the owner or user of the objects.

But colour impressions do not always correspond to the person's aura—they may quite possibly refer to a room of some particular colour, a dress, a mental visualisation of colour or some material connection. This can be ascertained by inquiry. The point to remember, however, is that colour is a symbol of soul-consciousness. The thoughts and emotions of a human being collect around the physical body in the form of fine vibrating waves or rays of colour.

There are seven major vibrating rays from which spring the seven basic types of human mentality and temperament ; in addition there are several minor rays.

The seven Major rays are :—

1. Violet,   Main characteristic—Spirituality.
2. Indigo,   Main characteristic—Intuition.
3. Blue,   Main characteristic—Religious Inspiration.
4. Green,   Main characteristic—Harmony and Sympathy.
5. Yellow,   Main characteristic—Intellect.
6. Orange,   Main characteristic—Energy.
7. Red,   Main characteristic—Life.

Each of these seven major rays is divided into many sub-hues. The Violet Ray, for example, is sub-divided into *Heliotrope, amethyst, orchid, royal purple, wisteria* and *lavender.*

As a general rule, clear bright colours symbolise *good* qualities, whilst dark, cloudy, mottled shades denote *bad* qualities. Pale, misty, pastel tints signify the highest or ethereal states of consciousness.

In the human aura there are basic colour-tones that reveal definite classes of talents, habits and character and there are numerous individual colour-tones.

Occult science teaches that there is a correspondence between colours and the human constitution. Most readers will be aware that every human being thinks and feels on differing planes of consciousness and that he possesses a vehicle or mode of expression for each plane, viz., the physical, astral mental and spiritual bodies. Each of these *bodies,* or forms of consciousness as they more correctly are, is related in some particular way to the three primary colours, *red*, *yellow*, and *blue*, which symbolise respectively :—

1. The Physical Body (physical—etheric)
2. The Soul (astral—mental)
3. The Spirit (higher mental—Spiritual)

From this trinity emanate or evolve the secondary or complimentary colours :—

Orange
Green
Indigo
Violet

From the foregoing principles it will be realised that there is a three-fold aura which corresponds to the three-fold human constitution. There is the physical aura, the astral-mental aura and the spiritual aura.

The following brief notes on the occult symbolism of colour will be of assistance to the student of psychometry.

Red. The symbol of life, strength and vitality.

The Physical Nature. Clear, bright red show generosity and ambition, also affection. An excess of red in the aura means strong physical propensities.

Dark Red—deep passion, e.g., love, courage, hatred, anger, etc., the dark cloudy shades are evil and sinister.

Reddish-Brown—sensuality, voluptuousness.

Very dark, rich tones—selfishness.

Cloudy red—greed and cruelty.

Crimson—lower passions and desires.

Scarlet—lust.

In contradistinction to these dark, earthly reds, there is the beautiful *rosy pink* the symbol of unselfish love.

Deep crimson—shot with black, gross materialism.

ORANGE.—The symbol of Energy.

The Etheric Nature.

Bright, clear orange—health and vitality.

Excess of orange in the aura indicates vital dynamic force.

Deep orange—pride.

Muddy, cloudy orange—low intellect.

YELLOW.—The symbol of Mind and Intellect.

The Mental Plane.

Golden yellow—high soul-qualities.

Pale primrose yellow—great intellectual power.

An excess of yellow in the aura shows an abundance of mental power.

Dark, dingy yellow—jealousy and suspicion.

Dull, lifeless yellow—false optimism, visionary mentality.

Gold present in the aura is a good sign.

GREEN.—The symbol of Harmony and Sympathy.

The Emotional Plane.

Bright clear greens—bespeak good qualities.

Light green—prosperity, success.

Mid green—adaptability, versatility.

An excess of green in the aura denotes individualism, supply, independence.

Clear green—sympathy.

Dark green—deceit.

Olive green—treachery, double-nature.

The dark shades are the more sinister.

BLUE.—The symbol of Inspiration and Devotion.

The Spiritual nature.

Deep clear blue—pure religious feeling.

Pale Eethereal blue—devotion to a noble ideal.

An excess of blue in the aura signifies an artistic, harmonious nature and spiritual understanding.

Bright blue—loyalty and sincerity.

INDIGO.—Symbol of the Mystic Borderland.

F

Indigo—symbolises spiritual attainment and self-mastery—wisdom and saintliness.

VIOLET.—The Symbol of Spirituality.

Deep purple—high spiritual attainment and holy love—the divine radiance.

Pale lilac and wisteria tints—cosmic consciousness and love for humanity.

Bluish-purple—transcendent idealism.

MINOR COLOUR MEANINGS.

Light grey—fear.

Dark grey—conventionalism, formality.

Heavy, leaden grey—meanness, lack of imagination.

Greyish-green—deceit, duplicity.

Brownish-grey—depression.

Black—malice, vice, depravity.

Pink—modesty, gentleness, unselfishness.

Silver—versatility, vivacity, movement.

An excess of silver in the aura is a sign of inconstancy and a fickle nature.

Light brown—practical mind.

Dull, grey-brown—selfishness.

Clear Brown—avarice.

In addition to colours, *symbols* frequently arise in connection with an object or person. Concisely speaking, a symbol is a thought-form expressing a relation between one plane and another, or in other words, an *objective* picture having a *subjective* meaning. Their interpretation is based upon the laws of thought and the correspondence that exists between the physical and the super-physical worlds.

It should be borne in mind that every symbol is capable of a threefold or fourfold interpretation depending upon the nature of the subject. The symbol may relate to the material, the astral, the mental or the spiritual planes. Thus a pair of scales would signify absolute justice on the spiritual plane, judgment or reason on the mental plane, emotional equilibrium on the astral plane, balance of forces or power in the physical. A pair of scales evenly balanced is a favourable sign, but if unequally balanced they denote a lack of harmony, mental balance or injustice.

Symbols may be divided into several groups, but the following main classifications will assist the student :—

1. Personal symbols
2. Animal symbols
3. Vegetable or plant symbols
4. Mineral symbols
5. Symbols of natural phenomena
6. Mechanical or artificial symbols

Among the first group we find such symbols as part of the body, clothes, common objects and so on. Thus *a hand* seen in a person's aura is symbolic of *flattery*, an eye symbolises the death of a friend or relative, and black beard indicates betrayal ; a foot signifies trouble and worries.

The symbolism of animals is very ancient and interesting. Since the days of Hermes Trismegistus, the vision of wild felines, or animals of monstrous shape, has been regarded as an evil omen, whilst all domestic animals, especially if of light colour (except the cat) are symbolic of good. Reptiles are the worst possible omens—they signify slander, vice and betrayal.

Fishes are good symbols—they portend abundance and wealth. Birds symbolise good or bad qualities according to their colour. Thus a blue bird means happiness, a white bird, peace and purity, a black bird, deceit and dishonour. A bat, which, of course, is not a bird, signifies mental or physical suffering and is sometimes given as a warning of danger. Bees symbolise the achievement of success through work, whilst a butterfly is a sign of in-constancy. An eagle is considered to be a sign of coming prosperity, whilst a gull betokens a safe journey. A frog symbolises a small indiscretion, and a grasshopper is an omen of impending loss.

Coming to the larger types of animals, a thin cow is symbolic of poverty, a healthy fat cow a sign of abund-ance and prosperity.

In many cases of psychometry and clairvoyance the symbol of a dog is given. The precise interpretation of this familiar creature will depend on the colour. Thus a white dog is an omen of happiness and friendship, a grey or black dog, an omen of disaster or misfortune, a yellow dog foretells serious calamity, a red dog is a portent of discord and strife. Generally speaking, unless they bear a distinctive colour, dogs are auspicious signs.

The domestic hen frequently occurs as a symbol and a variety of meanings are attached to it. If the hen is white it foretells gaiety and festivity, if black expect bad news, if noticeably fat then wealth is indicated, if thin, it shows lack of ambition. A number of hens seen in the aura is a sign of scandal and gossip.

Among the animal symbols expressing happiness and prosperity, are swans (white), sheep, swallows, rabbits and horses (if white) and also geese.

With regard to vegetable symbols, occultists down the ages seem agreed that they betoken evil and misfortune, with two exceptions, viz., mushrooms and peas. Green peas have frequently been seen in the aura of very happy and fortunate people, whereas symbols in the form of black beans have occurred in the aura of people facing grave dangers and perils. Mushrooms are a welcome symbol as they betoken life long and protection.

Flowers are a very common form of symbolism and their appearance is definitely good, with the exception of poisonous plants and certain green bushes, e.g., briar, bramble, cypress and holly.

The esoteric meaning of flowers depends in general upon their colours. Thus *red* flowers have some physical or material significance, blue flowers signify higher mental qualities, yellow flowers betoken wisdom and intellectual power. White flowers symbolise spiritual qualities.

The symbology of minerals and precious stones is interesting and extremely ancient. With the exception of *jet*, a good meaning is ascribed to each gem. Thus :—

Diamond signifies reconciliation, love
Amethyst signifies happiness, wealth
Jasper signifies courage, wisdom
Sapphire signifies truth
Emerald signifies hope, faithful love
Ruby signifies beauty, love of art
Opal signifies prayer, devotion
Turquoise signifies courage, hope
Pearl signifies purity
Amber signifies health

CHAPTER V

HUMAN PSYCHOMETRY AND PREDICTION

By human psychometry is meant the art of reading the memory-auras of human beings. A subject should be chosen about whom the psychometrist knows nothing or as little as possible. The subject should be encouraged to become physically and mentally tranquil, and should be comfortably seated with the legs uncrossed.

Standing close to the sitter, the psychometrist holds

his outstretched hands about six inches over the head—if there are any onlookers they should be at least five feet away. An assistant should keep a record of the readings and the subject's replies.

Results vary very much according to the type and temperament of the subject. After long and careful experiment it has been found that the best results are obtained from people belonging to the following groups :—

    1. The Intellectual
    2. The Emotional
    3. The Vital or vibrant type.

The psychometric phenomena arising from the above groups are more definite and so distinct than from subjects of less intelligence, less emotional nature, who are less vital.

It is interesting to note that the same results can be obtained from other parts of the body as well as the head. It makes no difference whether the hands are held six inches from the face, arms chest, back or legs. The reception of impressions, memory-pictures and so forth are as numerous and coherent as those obtained directly from the cranium.

This fact confirms the teaching of occult science that the mental and emotional auras are not localised in any particular region of the body but surround it in a fluidic circle.

After some amount of practice the psychometrist may find that he can dispense with the necessity of holding the hands over the subject's body. It will be found sufficient merely to concentrate the mind—without strain—upon the person to be psychometrised. Equally good results will be obtained as by the hand method.

An important factor in this form of psychometry is the distance between the subject and operator. Some operators are able to get the same results whether they are three feet or eight feet away—others are conscious of failure to psychometrise further than three or four feet from the subject. Care must be taken not to get beyond your right wave-length or sphere of receptivity.

Sometimes quite strange and remarkable phenomena occur in human psychometry. A psychometrist was once baffled by the appearance of a very strange and striking figure which manifested in the aura of a young lady subject. In fact, he hesitated mentioning it, but, true to the principles of the science, he went ahead and described what he saw.

"There is a strange figure with you—a short thick-set deformed person with a very forbidding-looking face. He is wearing rather odd and tattered clothes."

The lady smiled, " I think I can place him. I have just been reading the *Hunchback of Notre Dame*. You have just described the hunchback, Quasimodo."

The projection of thought-forms in the aura is quite a common occurrence in psychometry. The minds of most people are at all times in a state of incessant activity, creating images, recalling past events, expressing desires, building up hopes, and so on. They all flow into the auric stream and may be picked up by the psychometrist.

Another point to consider is that the mind never forgets. Incidents, events, everyday experiences which took place years ago may be seen and described. The sitter's conscious memory is not the only guide in deciding the accuracy of psychometric readings. Indeed, it is often a very unreliable source. The real storehouse of past experiences is the subconscious memory.

Everything in psychometry is based upon mind and thought. Thought is a creative force and people with a strong imagination (the mental image-making faculty) are able to endow the characters and scenes they read of in

books or see in films with life and individuality—living
thought-forms.   Such mental entities impinge on the
psychometrist's mind in the same way as the mental and
astral counterparts of real people and places. It is not easy
to distinguish one from the other.

The paramount importance of the mind and its inherent
phenomena brings us to the question of predicting the
future. If psychometry deals with the world of thought
to what dimensions may not the mind of the psychometrist
extend ? The field of psychometry is not bounded by
time and space.

According to J. W. Dunne in *Experiment with Time*
the mind works on a higher dimension than that of the
limited and separate states of consciousness known as
past, present and future. The mind transcends barriers
such as space—why should it not transcend time also ?

The extension of consciousness is a common phenomenon in the dream-state, in hypnotism and astral projection. Many people get prevision of the future in the
sleep-state and the power of certain people to make
correct predictions and forecasts whilst in the normal
waking consciousness is not to be denied.

The psychometrist who wishes to extend his readings
into the sphere of the unknown should first feel that he is
really and truly in the " conditions " or vibrations of the
sitter. Contacting the time-stream of the sitter is readily
achieved once the sensing of the person's vibration is
correctly done.   The right stage for extending the consciousness is reached when several correct statements have
been made concerning the past or the present state of the
sitter—this indicates that the psychometrist is properly
attuned to the sitter's vibration.

Warning should be given the sitter that an extension
into the future is proposed. The lifting of the veil occurs
either through concentration of the mind on the future

or through the extreme receptivity of the mind in which case the coming event casts its shadow without any conscious effort on the part of the psychometrist.

Sometimes a psychometrist gets a vision of a person, place, object, scene, etc. The sitter has no knowledge of such impressions neither can he recall them from his past experience. It may then be justly inferred that the impressions relate to the future. These readings, however, should not always be propounded or accepted as gospel truth. It sometimes happens that a psychometrist receives impressions from the reflecting ether (the imperishable records imprinted on the omnipresent ether) of the room. For example, a psychometrist described a room as being full of pictures and paintings of great beauty with a foreign atmosphere, and since the sitter had no knowledge of the place it was inferred that she would shortly be visiting an art gallery abroad. Some time later, however, it transpired that the room where the psychometric reading had been given had once been the studio of a distinguished French artist.

It should also be realised that it is possible for a psychometrist to predict his own future instead of the future of the sitter. Such instances have been known !

The ability to predict the future is not possessed by all psychometrists. Some sensitives, whose power to psychometrise in the ordinary way has been tested and proved, fail dismally in attempting to forecast the future. This is probably due to the fact that the mind of every psychometrist differs in some way or other either in vibration, structure or wave-length. Every practising psychometrist should study his own mind as well as the minds of other people. We live in a world of thought—we are constantly sending out and receiving thought-vibrations. Every day we add to the increasing and growing store of thoughts which make up the mental *aura*.

The basis of psychometry is the human mind and its field of activity is the amazing phenomena and power of the human mind. Not only does psychometry deal with the manifold activities of man's material mind but rightly used it leads us to the threshold of the Universal Mind and to an appreciation of the higher soul-qualities innate in every human being.

Mr. Ouseley will be glad to hear from readers on the subject of Psychometry and the Aura. Address letters to :— " Bracondale," Knoll Road, Dorking, Surrey.

($2\frac{1}{2}$d. stamp for reply.)

Society for Psychical Research.

Books by S.G.J. OUSELEY

Society for Psychical Research.

Books by S.G.J. OUSELEY

Telepathy — far feeling. p10

Printed in the United Kingdom
by Lightning Source UK Ltd.
105063UKS00001B/24

9 780766 130012